Always Face the Hounds:
The Negotiation for Osama bin Laden

By Meghan Hansen

ISBN-13:
978-1973864943

ISBN-10:
1973864940

"The supreme art of war is to subdue the enemy without fighting."

– Sun Tzu

Preface

Some stories are meant to be swept under the rug. They contain secrets buried in our hearts because some things are best forgotten, especially when lives are at stake. In the moment, we swear ourselves to secrecy and we commit to silence. Then, something happens, years later, and the story demands to be told in spite of the consequences and invasion of privacy. You hesitate knowing once the train has left the station, it's not coming backwards. When the cat gets out of the bag, it's out.

That's this story. This book is simply me recounting a week-long nightly conversation I had with a senior government official from the Middle East. Our talks were about gaining access for the United States to capture or kill Osama bin Laden, but our conversation took the road less traveled before I was able to argue for a sniper. In a way, this story is a missing piece of a puzzle in United States history. Maybe it's also a testament that a mere citizen with a strong will and a little bit of feistiness can make a difference. But even if I had confidence in that suggestion, it doesn't make this story any easier to tell because if telling it puts anyone at risk - it's me. Still, I know if this story is ever going to be told, now is the time.

The first time I hunted with the Galway Blazers in Ireland I was instructed, 'always face the hounds and never overtake the red coats (the hunter masters).' This was as true a sentiment for negotiating for the United States to gain access to capture or kill Osama bin Laden, the most wanted terrorist in the world. Carefully, I spoke only as a citizen; as a New Yorker on a mission, always staying behind the 'red coats' who would be able to change the international laws to finish this deal in Washington DC.

I never sought acknowledgement and I remain grateful to Secretary Hillary Clinton and President Barack Obama for leaving me out of the official story in 2011 as it certainly would have put me at risk at that time. Nobody would want to be the girl who negotiated the sniper to get bin Laden on the day after he was killed. That was the 'courier' or whomever else, but at least for a while it wasn't me. I was given the opportunity to be invisible and it was my choice not to come forward until now.

What happened in Abbottabad in May 2011, changed the world in one night, and let me say only this for Hillary Clinton: she didn't get enough credit and she deserves a tremendous round of applause from the entire world because dropping bombs and firing missiles are the easier way out. It doesn't take the same courage, strength, resolve or patience to drop a bomb than that which is required to sit face-to-face in front of someone you don't agree with, put yourself in their shoes, convince them that your agenda is a good idea for them and then change international laws in order to further that agenda and preserve innocent people's lives.

Changing international laws so that the United States could send a sniper team was not only the right thing to do, it's the right model to follow moving forward.

Americans do not want to see innocent civilians killed in America or in Pakistan or Afghanistan or Syria or Russia or any other countries. Innocent civilians are innocent civilians - we're only citizens without power no matter where we live. We're all in the same boat. Killing innocent people will not solve any problems or change the ideology of terrorists.

"Searching" for terrorists, as Donald Trump suggested we need to do, is also not the most intelligent way forward (how does anyone like looking for a needle in a large haystack?). Negotiating for terrorists is the way to go. Developing countries are desperate for aid from the United States, and there is so much good we can do if we can find ways to work together. We'd all rather be building schools than dropping bombs.

Even right now, we don't hate Russia or Russians. We hate Putin for bombing a playground, a school and a hospital in Syria, for targeting innocent civilians in the Ukraine, for holding corrupt and unfair elections in Russia, and for hacking the American election in 2016. If that's an 'Act of War' we should not be after Russia or Russians. Our country needs to target Putin, personally, like we took out Osama bin Laden. That does not mean we need to kill him, but perhaps, the United States can 'influence' the 2018 Russian election to return the favor.

Finally, please understand that I am not a politician. In fact, I really don't know much about politics. I've spent more than twenty years in the music business, and nothing in my professional life prepared me to negotiate with a leader in the Middle East to give up Public Enemy #1. Yet, somehow, at the time, I knew this accidental meeting was meant to happen, and although I was scared, I also knew that everything I had experienced in my life up to this moment led me to this.

Our meeting was not planned or intentional. I would never be so bold as to request a meeting with a leader or high-level government official or royalty of another country, not even the President running ours. My trip to Italy, which coincided with the opening ceremonies of the Olympics in Torino when many world leaders were in attendance, was purely meant to be a horseback riding / drag hunting trip (horses and hounds but no fox). However, for whatever reason, I was there, and he was there, and given that I am from NY and I can be a bit feisty as my Dad's cousin described me the other day when I was throwing a squatter off a family property in Ballintra, Ireland, of course, I had to ask,

"Why? Why would you let Osama bin Laden live in your country? Why won't you give him up to the United States?" And I opened a great big can of worms.

This book is not only about the negotiation for the United States to gain access to Osama bin Laden. It's also about asking questions; lots of questions. The reasons why the officials in Afghanistan and Pakistan wouldn't give up Osama bin Laden were a shocking surprise at first but not as much so after giving them some thought and hearing through the explanations and then conducting a little bit of research and consulting a few experts over the years.

When you first read this, it will sound far-fetched at best; when you start looking into it, you'll see otherwise.

Next, this is an interactive book, so please raise your hand if you remember where you were on 9/11?

Okay, that's everybody.

Now, if you were alive when John Lennon was killed in 1980, and you remember where you were, raise your hand.

Okay, that's everybody.

If you were alive when President John F. Kennedy was murdered, and you remember where you were when this tragedy happened, raise your hand.

Okay, that's everybody except George H.W. Bush.

Now, raise your hand if…

Why did you start raising your hand?

Hold that thought.

Arm yourself with a cup of coffee and Google and Wikipedia and as you go through this book, question everything and research, research, research. Try to stay with reliable sources for information like the *BBC, Guardian, New York Times, L.A. Times, or Washington Post* and make a special effort to look at international reporting – they do not have the same agenda as US media sources and often don't follow what our government would prefer they say. Also, look at sites that are written by freelance writers who write for major publications but have their own websites with more information – many are credible writers who have spent an incredible amount of time researching historical events.

In music, there are similar A&R talent acquisition methods – one bunch of people do the talent acquisition part of A&R like I do – they carefully, with their ears, screen new music and are incredibly picky about everything – artist, songs, arrangements, co-writers, presentation, and all else that goes into the vision and the artistry – and they only sign a couple of people at once who they know are artists worthy of the public's attention. Then, there is another way people do A&R – it's the 'sign everything around and throw it all up against a wall and hope a few stick' method – that method has worked for people as well. They are likely the reason 10% of the artists pay for the other 90%. And then, there's a method used by executives who only sign new artists based on research – these artists have a large social media presence and are getting tremendous airplay or have already sold 25,000 units of their demo on their own, and/or they can tour with very little tour support.

There are different ways to the same end, whether you are praying, signing talent or investigating a historical event. In President Kennedy's death, there are people who focus on doctored photographs, others who focus on the Warren Commission and their attempt to prove an untrue theory for the government that he was hit with a single bullet, still others who focus on Oswald who possibly didn't even have a gun that day – he was just the fall guy because he had been to Russia and the CIA apparently wanted to blame the Communists (sounds better than blaming themselves). And others look at those who had a motive and possibly conspired to kill the President. Are any of the investigations wrong?

Always keep an open mind, use your common sense and carry a grain of salt and a healthy dose of skepticism with you as you read. There are people you'll come across who were discredited by the CIA or the FBI because their stories concerning certain events don't match up with what the government wants the story to be (so they are going to discredit anything that doesn't confirm the details as they'd like them to have happened). For instance, James Files, who claims to have taken the shot that killed President Kennedy.

Search for James Files on YouTube. You tell me – is this man smart enough to have made up these details that happen to match up with key details of what happened that day? He answered question after question for over two hours. That would be a lot to remember if it wasn't the truth, especially for someone who isn't a member of any high IQ club.

Let me end with this: I'm only a citizen like you are and I have no power and no supernatural abilities to pull the truth out of the sky. I can only look at and listen to information and then use my experience and common sense to decide if I think it's credible, not credible or just ridiculous – and I strongly suggest you do the same.

It's been 11 years since I was in Italy and had this conversation and it's taken me all this time to adequately consider the information that was given to me by the gentleman I met.

It's not that I didn't find him credible – quite the opposite, I think the problem I've had all these years with this information is that he is exceptionally credible and happened to be at such a high level of government in a country that it was hard not to believe him – it's just that the information he conveyed to me was a shock to my system as I expect it will be to yours.

The conversation detailed in this book will not be retold exactly word-for-word. If you think back to a conversation you had 11 years ago, and recount it now, I'm sure you will have the same experience and would be able to relay information and context but not necessarily exact dialogue.

Finally, to clarify, I am not claiming to have been the first person to tell the United States government where Osama bin Laden was living in Abbottabad in 2006. They already knew where he was.

In fact, other people came forward including one gentleman who claimed to have told James Comey where Osama bin Laden was in Abbottabad, Pakistan in 2003. NBC covered the story here: *http://www.nbcnews.com/news/other/michigan-man-claims-he-told-us-where-bin-laden-was-f8C11517730*. What I did was help to negotiate the access so the United States could get to bin Laden to capture or kill him.

If, after you read these pages, you have a question you think I can answer, or you find a great resource you think I should share on the Always Face the Hounds Facebook page (www.facebook.com/alwaysfacethehounds), feel free to e-mail me at meghansen90265@gmail.com.

Very best,

Meghan Hansen
Malibu, California
May 2, 2017

Introduction

My life has always taken eccentric turns. Events and moments happen to me that never seem to happen to other people with 'normal' lives. But one thing I share with everyone is the impact losing my Dad had on my entire life and being.

When my Dad was very ill, I flew home to New York from California and ended up leaving my A&R position at Universal Music Group to spend time with him. A skin cancer lesion not caught soon enough leaked into his brain and the melanoma metastasized. He had three invasive brain surgeries, gamma knife surgeries and radiation procedures that eventually left him paralyzed on one side. It was heartbreaking for me to watch my Dad, who was truly everything to me, suffer while holding on to a glimmer of hope with the positivity he always had, that the next treatment would be the one that saves his life - but it didn't.

My Dad passed away at 57 years old and I was devastated.

Upon returning home to California, and back to work, I was ill. Very, very ill. Suddenly I had a 103 fever for over a week, rashes from head to toe including on my face and over my nose, cold sweats in bed at night and my eyes were extremely sensitive to light during the day. My boyfriend at the time insisted I see his doctor. The diagnosis was Lupus, an autoimmune disease. I cried all the way home.

The doctor said we can only treat the symptoms. There is no cure for Lupus. I don't do well on prescriptions; if there is a side effect to be had, I get it ten times worse than a normal person so I decided to refuse medication. He gave me a doctor's note for work and told me I could only work part-time until noon for a while. Within a few weeks, I couldn't even do that. I pushed myself anyway. I wanted to be healthy again and I wanted to be at work like everyone else.

And then my heart gave up. It was an intense life moment and I was grateful to survive. While I was recovering for several weeks, I pulled together my bucket list and I was in a rush. I didn't know how soon until I was out of time.

I've been riding horses my entire life (since I was 5) and I always wanted to hunt with the Galway Blazers in Ireland. It's not the easiest hunt, so to be safe, I decided to go warm up for a week and ride in a drag hunt in Italy first.

When I arrived, hotel staff asked if they could do an international background check on me. I said that was fine, and only had to wonder why for a couple of hours.

Later that afternoon, the barn lady pointed out a man on the property with whom I would be hunting that week, and she told me he is a senior government official from the Middle East named ADIR (not his real name). I said, "he must not like Americans; please introduce me as an Irish girl." But the head of the equestrian facility had already told him I live in California.

What he didn't know yet was that I'm originally from New York City and like anyone else from New York, I had a grudge against the Middle East. I asked him, "Why would you let Osama bin Laden live in your backyard? Why won't you give him up to the United States? Why won't you let America bring him to justice?"

For the entire week, we talked and I listened to what I thought were some of the wildest points and objections to giving up Osama bin Laden to the United States. After years in the music business, I thought I'd heard just about everything, but nothing like this.

Adir was well-spoken, exceptionally intelligent, kind-hearted, and very educated. His English was good, and he was overall a formidable opponent to argue with. It was an honor to have this opportunity and I'm grateful he gave me the chance to express myself. He listened and made every attempt to understand where I was coming from as a citizen of the United States. When we parted, it was on good terms, but I didn't keep in touch because the Bush Administration put me on the "Do Not Fly" list. I can take a hint.

In the pages that follow, I'll walk you through the week-long conversation I had with Adir. Judge the information for yourself. This isn't a researched-for-you history book. Instead, this is a do-your-own-research adventure because that's the only way you'll believe any of this.

THE CONVERSATION

It was my first evening in the hotel restaurant. I was sitting at the bar and Adir came in and joined me. We moved to a quiet corner, away from other guests, and began our lengthy talks that would extend through the week.

Our conversation was relaxed and friendly. I learned about the Middle East, key historic facts, places to visit someday when it's safe, and then we turned to the topic at hand. Why would the leaders in the Middle East allow Osama bin Laden to live in their backyard?

I described the impact of 9/11 on citizens in New York and he outlined why the leaders in the Middle East objected to giving bin Laden up to the United States. He made several key points and brought up some hair-raising questions.

1: Osama bin Laden was not the mastermind behind the attacks on the United States on September 11th, 2001.

Nobody will ever forget the morning of September 11, 2001. I watched those tragic moments of the World Trade Center towers falling in New York over and over on television from California. It looked as if the city I had moved from was turned into a war zone. Nearly 3,000 people were killed, about 3,000 kids were left without a parent, first responders were killed, others were injured for life, and for weeks, people walked the streets with photos of missing family members who weren't found yet hoping for a miracle they didn't get. It was the most horrific attack on American soil in the history of the United States.

And now, here I was, a girl originally from New York, born in the city, sitting in front of a high-level government official in the Middle East and I couldn't believe he and the other leaders in the Middle East would not give up Osama bin Laden to the United States. How dare they let him live there? In my mind, it wasn't optional – they needed to give this monster up and they needed to do it now.

"You know where he is, right?" I asked.

"Yes, and so does your government," Adir answered.

"Where is he?"

"Abbottabad in Pakistan. Not too far from Islamabad," he said. "Near the military academy."

"Does the Pakistan military know he is there?"

"High-ranking officers do."

"How long has he been there?"

"Several years."

"Who does he live with?" I asked.

"His five wives and family."

I laughed. "He lives in one house with five wives and kids? Most of my male friends would think that's a form of torture, probably worse than jail."

Adir laughed too. "In our religion, we can have five wives."

"So, if I switch religions, can I have five husbands? I'm not so sure I want so many. That seems like a lot of work!"

Adir laughed. "It doesn't work that way, but I don't personally want five wives. You're right. It's a lot."

"Are you sure the United States knows bin Laden is in Abbottabad and they know exactly where to find him?"

"Yes, but the Bush administration doesn't want to get him," Adir said. "They wouldn't take him even if we handed him over on a platter."

"Americans want to get him," I told him. "Our media shows him in a cave in Afghanistan, not in good health, receiving medical treatment while we have thousands upon thousands of troops on the ground looking for him. I personally never found that story believable. He's in Pakistan?"

"Yes, however, they are correct that he is not in good health," Adir said. "They should not be reporting that he's in Afghanistan. He hasn't been there in years."

"I understand, but the way the media works is that he could be walking around the streets in New York and as long as the media places him in Afghanistan, he's there in Americans' minds," I said. "In many ways, it's true that perception is more important than the truth in America."

"So, your people don't know the truth?"

"We only know what the television news and newspapers tell us. It's certainly not the level of information that someone like you, a higher up in government would have. It's limited information at best," I said. "It's only what the government wants us to hear, however true or untrue. And sometimes it seems late or incomplete or as if someone was playing the telephone game when the last person who hears the story gets to tell it, however mangled it is at that point."

"The telephone game?" Adir looked amused.

"It's a game we all played in school as kids. We sat in a circle, and the teacher whispered something to one kid, then that kid whispered it to the next kid, and so on until we were at the end of the circle. The last kid announced what he thought the message was. Rest assured, by then it wasn't quite what the teacher told the first kid, if it even resembled the original whisper at all. That's kind of how we get our information in America."

I continued, "The government tells the media what they want us to hear, then it gets filtered through the media outlets, then if they see it fit to print, it gets broadcast or written about after it's gone through more people. By the time it gets to the public, they probably get it right most of the time, parts of it right some of the time, and sometimes it just goes out the window. Anyone with common sense can see it didn't quite happen that way or there's more to the story that may or may not change whether what was broadcast was totally accurate. So what you know from being in government is more than any private citizen would know."

"That's good to know that the messages I receive are not the same messages you receive," Adir said. "It would help to see your media."

I circled back to the subject at hand.

"Why does the Bush administration not want to find bin Laden?" I asked this curiously as I was recalling Bush publicly stating that he wasn't really looking for bin Laden anymore, only about 6 months after 9/11. That stunned me and many other people I knew.

Adir answered, "Osama bin Laden was not the mastermind behind 9/11. If you think back, at first he denied any involvement in the September 11th attacks only to later bask in the limelight of public attention for being the world's most wanted terrorist. It's not that he's completely innocent, but he was not behind the attacks in America.

"The Taliban offered to give him up if the Bush administration could show proof that he was behind the attacks, and there wasn't proof, and Bush didn't want him anyway."

[YouTube: Bin Laden Releases Statement Denying Responsibility for 9/11 Attacks
https://www.youtube.com/watch?v=NPn-IdeN85s]

Adir paused for a few moments and then said, "He's not as clever as he thinks he is."

"I'd bet on that one, but if the mastermind behind 9/11 wasn't bin Laden, who was the terrorist-in-chief?"

"Do you understand the relationship between the Bush and bin Laden families?" He changed the subject as far as I could tell.

"No," I said.

2. Bush had no interest in capturing or killing Osama bin Laden.

Here's a quick synopsis of what Adir told me: George H.W. Bush and members of Osama bin Laden's family have been business partners for many years. Further, Salem bin Laden, Osama's older brother, was one of George W. Bush's first business partners. The bin Ladens' financed George W. Bush's first business ventures including his oil company, Arbusto Energy oil company in Texas. Even though Salem died in a small plane crash in 1988, Bush was still tied to his family, and it's no wonder Bush didn't want to direct a manhunt for his close friend and financier's brother. *[YouTube: News footage of George W. Bush saying he's not focused on finding bin Laden: https://www.youtube.com/watch?v=4PGmnz5Ow -o]*

Adir also noted that Osama bin Laden worked for the CIA when George H.W. Bush was the director. Bush was in a meeting with Osama bin Laden's brother on 9/11, and the Bush and bin Laden families were so close that even when all planes were grounded because of 9/11, George W. Bush arranged for the bin Laden family to leave the United States for Saudi Arabia without being questioned by our intelligence agencies.

Still glued to my seat in the corner of the bar, sitting across from Adir, I took a sip of water, and then asked, "Is Saudi Arabia paying for him to be in Abbottabad?"

"The Saudi's are angry with him. He's not getting any money, and he no longer has citizenship."

"Who is paying for him then?" I asked.

He looked at me, and I recalled my Dad who used to tell me not to ask a question if I'm not ready to hear the answer.

3. The US went to war for the oil. It wasn't about revenge for 9/11.

"It makes no sense for the United States to be after the oil in Afghanistan and Iraq because it's only enough to sustain America for a few more decades," Adir said.

He went on to say the Afghanistan war was planned in the summer of 2001, before the September attacks. The Bush Administration wanted to work with the Taliban to develop oil resources and construct a pipeline. When negotiations with the Taliban fell apart, it became a military operation instead of an energy initiative and business deal. Finally, the Bush Administration gave the Taliban an ultimatum: Accept the offer or expect bombs.

"9/11 was caused by people inside of America," Adir said. "Do you understand?"

"Automation would prevent hijackers from taking over planes," he said. "Also, if you look at other buildings that have been hit by planes, they fall sideways, not straight down like a controlled demolition. In addition, if you re-watch the videos of the Trade Center coming down, you can see little explosions," he told me. "How would someone get explosives into the World Trade Center and up several floors? It wouldn't be a terrorist; it would be someone on the inside.

"Explosives explain Building 7 falling straight down, too. That building, which contained thousands of intelligence records, was not hit by a plane," he said. Then he noted that Bush's brother and cousin were heads of the company that provided security for the World Trade Center.

Adir went on to explain that the hijackers were not real. The original passenger lists did not list any Arab passengers, but he said the FBI fixed it. A couple of the listed passengers were dead before 9/11 and a few more were still alive after the attacks.

At this point, I must have looked completely shocked. Even though I had seen Michael Moore's documentary *Fahrenheit 9/11*, I wasn't fast to buy the '9/11 is an inside job' theory. I wasn't convinced before, and I still had questions, but now, listening to Adir, I was floored.

I had a lot to ask. Did Bush know the attacks were coming and ignore the warnings? Or did he have a hand in creating the 9/11 attacks to gain public support for his planned war for oil? Adir clearly thought it was the latter, but I wasn't convinced. All I knew was that 9/11 should be reinvestigated.

The "War on Terrorism" is not a war on anyone else if any of the culprits that caused 9/11 live at high-end addresses in the United States of America.

4. Should the President of the United States and his family profit from war or be financially incentivized to go to war?

It was another rainy evening in Italy. I thought I was early getting to the corner of the bar, but Adir was already waiting for me.

"Have you heard of the Carlyle Group? Are you aware of what they do?" Adir asked me.

"Probably not entirely," I said. "But the Carlyle Group was mentioned in the *Fahrenheit 9/11* movie."

"I heard that's a conspiracy theory movie. I don't watch those," Adir said. "Does it show what the wars did to Afghanistan and Iraq? To the innocent civilians there?"

"I think the movie was dedicated to them," I said. "Adir, most Americans don't want civilians in Afghanistan or Iraq to live in a war zone as they have for so many years, just like we don't want to live in a war zone.

We want to help them. And to some of us, it seems like we went to war in Iraq to take the attention off Bush not wanting or not being able to get bin Laden. Our country has a lot to make up for."

"It's your President and his family, and their greed."

I nodded.

Adir explained that the Carlyle Group – dubbed "The Ex-Presidents Club," – is a large private equity and investment firm whose investors included the bin Laden and the Bush families. George H.W. Bush was an officer of the company until he was forced to step down after 9/11 due to conflict-of-interest concerns.

The Carlyle Group is believed to have more political ties than the White House – a de facto extension of the government. Its offices are located on Pennsylvania Avenue in Washington D.C. between the White House and the Capitol Building. In 2001, the Carlyle Group had extensive holdings in the defense/arms manufacturing industry and national security markets including United Defense, Inc. They acquired controlling interests in several underperforming defense contractors and used their political rolodex to land big Pentagon contracts. Then they would sell their interest in the companies to other investors at a huge profit.

Adir said the Carlyle Group essentially caused 9/11 to generate the necessary public support for a war in Afghanistan the Bush Administration had already planned. It would be a war that would not only create a demand for arms, but also enable Bush to pursue his oil pipeline agenda. Two birds, one stone.

Adir went on to talk about Cheney's Halliburton, one of the world's largest oil drilling companies. They stood to gain billions from wars in Afghanistan and Iraq and were partnered with none other than the Saudi bin Laden Group, the largest construction company in the world.

The Carlyle Group and Halliburton are the link between the Afghanistan and Iraq wars and the personal pocketbooks of politicians – not the least of which were the father of the current President of the United States and his Vice President.

Remember that old saying? Follow the money.

"It's interesting that you didn't watch *Fahrenheit 9/11*," I said to Adir. "Everything you've told me so far matches up with the movie although the movie doesn't have so many details."

"Have a lot of people watched it in America?" He asked.

"Yes, it's the most watched, highest grossing documentary of all time." In 2006, it was.

5. *The United States created the Taliban*

Adir and I continued to talk and he explained how the United States created the Taliban to fight the Soviet Union during the Cold War. Here's a synopsis:

In the 70s and 80s, the United States was engaged in the Cold War with the Soviet Union. When the Soviet Union invaded Afghanistan, the U.S. intervened because it didn't want the Soviet Union to take control of Central Asia and gain more power. The United States partnered with the Pakistani intelligence agency (ISI) and supplied billions of dollars, weaponry, and logistical help to recruit military officers with extreme views of Islam in the fight against the Soviet Union. This military is now known as the Taliban, and they successfully drove the Soviets out of Afghanistan by the end of the 1980s.

After the war, Afghanistan and Pakistan were left unaided to deal with the postwar mess. Because the Taliban was created by the Pakistani intelligence agency, many Pakistani military officers and others side with the Taliban.

Soon after the 9/11 attacks, the U.S. declared war against Afghanistan and the weapons once designated to fight the Soviets were turned against us. The Taliban then turned against their own country, destroying landmarks and sacred places and creating an internal civil war.

What does it mean that the Taliban are extremists and distort their own religion? Remember David Mitchell, the crazy man who kidnapped and raped Elizabeth Smart in the name of the Bible? I don't own that version of the Bible, and hopefully, you don't either. That's distorting Catholicism in the same way the Taliban distorts Islam. Allah does not want dead Americans, and God doesn't want to kill anybody in the Middle East. In fact, Adir and I compared notes and we concluded that all the religions pretty much say the same thing. It comes down to the Golden Rule: Do unto others as you would have them do unto you. In other words, what goes around comes around.

Saudis, Afghans, and Pakistanis want Americans to feel comfortable to come and visit their countries, to see historical sites, and to enjoy the experience of traveling. But in 2006, the U.S. media was telling Americans that Osama bin Laden was in Afghanistan, and Americans don't want to visit Middle Eastern countries inclined to harbor our nation's Public Enemy #1 or do business with terrorists (as is rumored with Saudi Arabia). Plus, terrorists were cutting people's heads off and posting graphic videos on the Internet in 2006.

Understandably, a vacation package to these parts of the Middle East is one that most people chose to avoid, thinking it wiser to stay a world away.

6. *George H.W. Bush was responsible for the assassination of President John F. Kennedy.*

"So even if Bush had full access to get bin Laden, they have no interest in bringing him to justice?" I asked Adir, steering him back to George Bush.

"No, and we won't give him access," he said.

"Who won't give the United States access? Afghanistan and Pakistan will not work with the Bush Administration?"

"No. Do you understand what kind of people they are? How did he get elected twice?" Adir seemed frustrated, even angry.

"I have no idea. I didn't vote for him," I said. "He didn't win the popular vote either time and please remember, the United States has over 300 million people in it. Some of us are brilliant and some of us are stupid as a rock, and most are in between. Some people voted for George Bush, most of us didn't. It's the antiquated electoral college that elected him. I wish they'd do away with it."

"Don't Americans realize that your electoral college, the way it is presently used, contradicts your own Constitution?" Adir asked. "If 1 person = 1 vote, then how come a person in Wyoming's vote means so much more than a person in New York? That's unconstitutional by your own law."

"It's probably the Republicans' last chance," I suggested. "Since their platform no longer reflects the views of the majority of the people in the United States, they don't get elected without a lot of help."

"They steal elections. According to the United States Constitution, Gore should be the President of the United States." Adir insisted.

"I agree. The Republicans stole the election in 2000 not only because of the electoral college being unfair and disproportionate in its count but also because Ohio and Florida were employing some very creative vote accounting methods. Those Ohio voting machines are famous now."

"Everyone watches America," Adir said. "Every single country and their leaders. How could the citizens in the United States be okay with such an unfair system? How could they just stand by and watch? Don't the citizens in your country demand answers?"

"We can demand anything we want, but citizens in the United States really don't have any power. Neither do citizens in Italy, where we are now. Neither do citizens in Saudi Arabia or Pakistan or Afghanistan or Iran. We probably have more freedoms, but we don't have much more say. All civilians are pretty much in the same boat. Powerless."

Adir countered, "But you've had leaders who care about citizens like you."

"Who are you referring to?"

"When I was younger, I went to the White House. President Kennedy invited us. My family met with the President and he was a very, very kind man. He was a friend, truly a good friend."

Adir paused for a moment and showed me a picture of a gift he received from President Kennedy. I said I'd love to see it, and he immediately invited me to visit him in the Middle East. I was struck by his graciousness.

I could tell as Adir was relaying his story, that this trip to the White House meant everything to him. It was one of the highlights of his life. He still had a powerfully strong loyalty to President Kennedy and his family.

Adir went on to tell me that a top-level CIA officer told him that George H.W. Bush had planned the assassination of President Kennedy. Because of that, he said no one in the Middle East would consider giving the Bush administration access to Osama bin Laden even if Bush would take him.

I was stunned. "Why?" I asked, all the while thinking to myself, you could not make this stuff up.

Here's what I remember of what Adir told me. Prescott Bush was a director for a financial company that managed finances for the Nazis including Adolf Hitler *[For more information: The Guardian: https://www.theguardian.com/world/2004/sep/25/usa.secondworldwar]*.

Prescott went on to run Nixon's unsuccessful campaign against Kennedy. George H.W. Bush and his father's friend, E. Howard Hunt were supervisors in the CIA under Bush's long-time friend,

Director Allen Dulles. They were assigned to the Bay of Pigs invasion in 1961.

After the Cuban Revolution, Fidel Castro embraced economic ties with the Soviet Union during its Cold War with the United States. President Dwight Eisenhower, in turn, wanted to overthrow Castro's regime and allocated more than $13 million dollars to the CIA to oust Castro from power with the assistance of CIA operatives and counter-revolutionary Cuban forces.

When the CIA sought President John F. Kennedy's approval of air cover for the mission, he denied it. But the CIA mission went ahead anyway, even though it was impossible to succeed without air cover.

The operation failed, not only causing embarrassment to George H.W. Bush but also proving counterproductive to his father's interests. Worse, the failure strengthened relations between Cuba and the Soviet Union, which eventually led to the Cuban Missile Crisis of 1962. President Kennedy famously went against the CIA and ordered several internal investigations.

George H.W. Bush, for many years, could not remember where he was when President Kennedy was assassinated, but photos and an unclassified FBI memo show that he was in Dallas, Texas that day. Adir told me Oswald was not the shooter. In fact, he was told Oswald wasn't even a good shot, and the CIA knew that. But Oswald had been to Russia and the CIA wanted to blame the communists. Jack Ruby killed Oswald so he couldn't talk. Adir said the real killer is "still out there" but George H.W. Bush is responsible.

George H.W. Bush had seemed like a likeable guy to me —a veteran and a lifelong Republican like my Dad. I'm not a Republican and would never vote for a Bush, but was he really a murderer? Of course, in every good movie, the villain tends to have a few good qualities or accomplishments. But this was not a movie and I didn't know what to make of this information impossible for me to independently verify.

Whether what Adir said was true or not, I knew right then that there was no way on earth that he or his colleagues would give up Osama bin Laden to the United States in 2006 or until Bush left office. My heart sank. Up until now, this conversation was going well and I thought I could possibly turn the tide of history. And now, it was turning out to be an impossible feat.

As if all this wasn't enough, Adir said, "but that's not it…"

"Oh, God," I thought, "What on earth else?"

"Have you heard of the Order of Skull & Bones, the Yale Club?"

"I heard it's an elite secret society at Yale in New Haven that is called 'Bones' for short and members are called 'Bonesmen.'" I paused so Adir finished.

Adir told me that Skull & Bones is a club in which members are sworn to secrecy after sharing secrets about terrible acts they have committed. For example, it's rumored Prescott Bush was one of the grave diggers who stole Geronimo's skull, bones, and horse's bridle. Each man has done something equally as terrible as the next guy so no one talks, and the club stays intact.

Just thinking about it made me nervous, but Adir's next question threw me off.

Adir asked, "You love music?"

"Yes, and I always have. I love all kinds of music," I replied.

"Did you like the Beatles?"

"They were my Dad's favorite band," I said. I've been singing along to Beatles songs on 45s since I was 1. I love them. I still listen to them. What about you?"

"I didn't like them. They were too popular, too mainstream."

"I think you might be the only person on this planet who didn't love the Beatles."

Adir smiled and continued.

"They weren't as popular in my country, but I remember their songs," he said. "They are simple songs like 'Let It Be.' I can sing it. Is that why people liked them so much?"

"Yes, memorable songs definitely write your ticket in the music business but the Beatles weren't only memorable. They were unforgettable," I said. "And John Lennon stood for something: Peace."

"That's what killed him. Do you understand what happened to John Lennon?"

I replied, "He was murdered by a man named Mark David Chapman when I was 6 years old. I remember standing at the television set, and I told my Dad I thought someone told him to do that but what did I know? I was only 6."

"You were right. Have you ever heard of the CIA's Project MK ULTRA?"

"No."

Adir explained, "It was the CIA's mind control program. Director Allen Dulles formed it and hired Dr. Sidney Gollieb to run it. They took the idea from the Nazis and hired some of their scientists. Their goal was to use the techniques on the Soviets the way the Soviets, the Chinese and North Koreans were using them on U.S. prisoners of war.

"They would give participants a cocktail of drugs including LSD for about a week and then hypnotize them to assassinate or spy on someone on command. The participant would forget everything (necessary if they were captured by an enemy) and then only remember by seeing or hearing a specific cue. They also wanted to figure out a way to get someone to confess what they know against their will. And they wanted to be able to erase their mind. The CIA did these experiments on U.S. citizens often without their knowledge or consent."

"Wow, that sounds frightening."

"Have you read *The Catcher in the Rye?*" Adir asked.

"Not recently," I replied. "Maybe I read it in junior high school, but I don't remember it. It's one of those books that you read once, write a book report, and never read it again. *To Kill a Mockingbird, Adventures of Tom Sawyer, The Great Gatsby, Of Mice and Men* and

20 other books are all like that too. Nobody holds on to those books.”

“Every American has read *The Catcher in the Rye*?”

“Most do, if they went to junior high school. Why?”

“It’s a trigger.”

“For what?”

“Assassination. That’s why schools in the United States banned the book for several years.”

“Assassination of whom?” I must have looked horrified.

“George H.W. Bush had John Lennon killed and was responsible for the Reagan shooting. Then John F. Kennedy, Jr., when he was about to expose George H.W. Bush as the man who had his father killed, died in a plane crash with his wife, her sister, and a mystery flight instructor who was not named. George W. Bush was seen near the hangar and was missing for 3 days but nobody had any questions for him. They even searched in the wrong place at first.

"The Skull & Bones Club also had Robert Kennedy killed, Martin Luther King, Jr., and a 13-year-old little girl killed. Do you remember Samantha Smith? She was from Maine, a peace activist known as 'America's Youngest Ambassador.' Today, she would be a couple of years older than you, and there is something about you that is a lot like her. How could anyone kill a little girl like that? She was only a baby. She wanted peace and your government killed her. Skull & Bones were also responsible for the attempted assassinations of Gerald Ford and George Wallace and there were more. All of the killers were programmed through mind control programs like MK ULTRA. Americans don't know this?"

I was shocked.

"This isn't what we see on our evening news or learn about in history classes in the United States," I said. "But to be honest, if a mentally ill young man or woman shoots, or even shoots at (Adir did mention there was another shooter in at least two of these cases and when you look online you'll find people discuss information about forensics that confirm this) a famous politician who would be our next President, Robert Kennedy, or an artist like John Lennon, it does seem like a very convenient defense to say, 'I was mind control programmed and therefore I am not responsible.'

"Besides," I asked, "why would anyone want to kill John Lennon? I get why George H.W. Bush would want President Reagan out of the way: to become President. But why John Lennon?"

"John Lennon had a lot of power," Adir said. The FBI and the CIA stalked him because they were afraid of him. His idea of foreign policy did not match Bush's agenda for foreign policy, and it was a problem for Bush that John Lennon had a big mouth and millions and millions of followers. He had his own agenda for peace and against war, and he could easily inspire a million people or more to protest within about an hour."

I shook my head. "It broke the entire world's heart to lose him."

I have a basic knowledge of mind control and hypnosis because I have a close friend of many years who is a best-selling author in the field. But still, I had to take a moment to think about this. Were these killers truly lone wolves who carried out assassinations for their own reasons, or were they victims of the political system themselves?

Adir pointed out that if you look at just one of these 'lone wolf' incidents, it makes sense that hypnosis and mind programming could seem like a made-up excuse for one's murderous actions. However, if you examine the assassinations together as a group, you'll notice there are eerie commonalities. You at least have to wonder why Mark David Chapman, Jack Ruby, John Hinckley, Jr., James Earl Ray, Robert John Bardo, Arthur Bremer, and Sirhan Sirhan all had a copy or quoted from *The Catcher in the Rye* – Like a Jack of Diamonds in "*The Manchurian Candidate?*"

Of all books out there, why would everybody have that one? Is the cover of the book a hypnosis trigger? Or is it the Skull & Bones signature? Or both? It certainly is not the book itself. I can't imagine a mind control subject having to read an entire book in order to perform a task of any magnitude, let alone an assassination. If that was the requirement, I bet nobody would ever get killed.

Don't take my word for it – research it yourself online. When Robert John Bardo killed actress Rebecca Schaeffer, according to Wikipedia, "He visited her at her apartment and told her he was a big fan. She signed an autograph, went back into her apartment and he left. About an hour later, Bardo again rang the bell to her apartment. Upon Schaeffer opening the door, Bardo fired one round of ammunition, killing her." What does that mirror? That's the same scenario as John Lennon's death.

In AP news footage, George Wallace suggested his shooter, Arthur Bremer, did not act alone and he questioned how someone with little means had money for travel, expensive hotel rooms, limos, and guns. He also noted that Bremer kept a diary like Sirhan Sirhan but had never kept a diary in his life until then.

You can search YouTube for the footage or type in this link: *[George Wallace Suggests Shooter was Part of a Conspiracy: https://www.youtube.com/watch?v=FAxB9WYJN_Q]*

Who else kept a diary? Mark David Chapman among several of the others. Who else had unexplained financial resources for travel, etc.? Take a wild guess.

A 1979 ABC News Special called "Mission Mind Control: MK ULTRA & the CIA" offers more background into the MK ULTRA program. Search on YouTube or type in this link: *https://archive.org/details/ABCNews_MissionMindControl-CIA_and_MKULTRA*

Even more chilling to listen to is the end of Robert Kennedy's last speech. Search for it on YouTube or type in this link: *https://www.youtube.com/watch?v=ae7H0aWFWNY* . The chant, "Kennedy, Kennedy Ra Ra Ra" was not a typical presidential rally shout, but more likely a unique hypnosis trigger. Notice as soon as it is chanted, you hear a shot.

That's not all. Check out this BBC article: _http://news.bbc.co.uk/2/hi/programmes/newsnight/6169006.stm_

And, Project MK ULTRA on Wikipedia: _https://en.wikipedia.org/wiki/Project_MKUltra_ – scroll down to the "Hypnosis" section, and you'll see that Dr. Sidney Gollieb discovered and tested the use of keyword trigger programming. When the patient was programmed to accept specific key words, the agenda of the programmer could be carried out.

Even more information can be found on the WhoWhatWhy.org website by searching for MK ULTRA or by typing this link into your browser: _https://whowhatwhy.org/2016/04/29/government-mind-control-agent-talks/_

MK ULTRA stands for "Manufacturing Killers Utilizing Lethal Tradecraft Requiring Assassinations." To dig deeper, search for "MK ULTRA Subproject 140" or "MK ULTRA Subproject 3" online.

All of these 'lone wolf' shooters sold to the public as mentally ill, angry stalkers were reportedly calm after each shooting. That's interesting. And, some of what the killers said right after the shooting was reportedly the same – for a bunch of mentally ill misfits, presumably unknown to one another, it's hard to believe they would come out with the same rhetoric. So when you read about these assassinations, watch for commonalities not only in the manner of the crimes themselves but also in the responses of the killers. Did Arthur Bremer, James Earl Ray, Mark David Chapman and others say they wanted to be famous in the same way? That's not a coincidence. That's programming.

If you look online you'll also find connections have been drawn between Chapman's behavior and those of other 'lone wolf' killers or attempted killers, particularly John Hinckley, who attempted to assassinate President Ronald Reagan and had a copy of *The Catcher in the Rye*. John Hinckley's father was a close friend of George H.W. Bush, and was president of a company called World Vision, where Chapman was employed. Adir said some of the CIA "mind control camps" were run under the umbrella of this organization. Whether or not this information is accurate is up for grabs, but as Americans, I think we deserve a re-investigation of these assassinations or assassination attempts and certainly the victims deserve justice.

Reportedly, President Ford let slip information that the CIA had been involved in conspiracies to assassinate political leaders. According to Wikipedia (Daniel Schorr's entry), "on May 14, 2006, on NPR's *Weekend Edition*, Schorr mentioned a meeting at the White House that took place with colleague A. M. Rosenthal and president Gerald Ford. Ford mentioned that the Rockefeller Commission had access to various CIA documents, including those referring to political assassinations."

Obviously, we can't talk with President Ford now, but George H.W. Bush is still alive as I'm writing this. How about Congress asks him a few questions?

Can anyone 'un-program' an MK ULTRA mind control participant? Once their mission is completed or attempted, will they still respond to the same mind control trigger(s)? For instance, before Arthur Bremer tried to kill George Wallace, he wanted to kill President Nixon. His obsession apparently could be transferred with the same specific trigger(s). Same with Robert John Bardo who originally set out to kill Samantha Smith and then changed his obsession to Rebecca Schaeffer and murdered her. Furthermore, John Hinckley reportedly stalked Jimmy Carter in the years before shooting President Ronald Reagan. If the United States does not un-program these people, aren't they always going to be a risk?

There are likely only a handful of people in the world who can help retrieve memories of someone who was subject to MK ULTRA mind programming. I consulted with an internationally recognized expert in hypnosis: Dr. Shelley Stockwell-Nicholas, President of the International Hypnosis Federation, and she told me, "Someone mind programmed (i.e. via the CIA's MK ULTRA program) can recover exact memories of what happened to them using hypnosis. It may require one or more sessions depending on the rapport with the hypnotist. Brainwashing utilizes what we call the hypnotic seal and the seal is broken with rapport and contact with the person's higher all-knowing self." Dr. Shelley is open to work independently or with other experts to help deprogram clients. She is reachable via e-mail at shelleynicholas@cox.net.

In the Preface, if you were alive for 9/11, John Lennon's murder, and President Kennedy's assassination, did you raise your hand four times? This is something hypnotists refer to as a "yes set" - ask someone three questions they'll say "yes" to and then ask a fourth question and most people will say "yes" without thinking about it. Hypnosis is not necessarily complicated. MK Ultra mind programming is more intricate than this example, but likely not as complex as most of us would think, and the good news is, as Dr. Shelley said, it's possible for someone who was mind programmed to be deprogrammed and remember.

At this point in my conversation with Adir, it was about 1:30am in Italy. This was a lot for me to digest, and I was getting tired.

"Where did you get this information?" I finally asked, nervously.

"A senior-level officer, a top person in the CIA," Adir said. He identified the source and said he was a friend, but I don't recall the name.

Adir shared his insights as if I should have known them already, as if I missed a bunch of history classes in high school or college. The truth, however, is that I'm a bit of a geek. I didn't miss anything, not one minute. I graduated the New School for Social Research in New York with a Bachelor of Arts and a 3.9/4.0 GPA. It's just that nobody teaches *this* version of history!

Even if I had access to a computer that night, the Internet was limited in 2006, and I still would have been shocked by what Adir told me. I think most Americans would feel the same way.

After leaving Adir at the bar that evening, I considered leaving for Ireland early and forgetting about Osama bin Laden. I could tell my friends the story of how 'I tried' but this negotiation was like getting over the Great Wall of China that keeps growing bigger. And the Kennedy assassination was personal to him and I didn't feel I could get past it.

I fought with myself the entire night. Should I leave for Ireland in the morning? Something in me felt I could pull off a miracle so for better or for worse, I stayed.

7. The United States will send a missile or a bomb and kill innocent civilians in Pakistan if we allow them access to Osama bin Laden.

I walked into the bar smiling. It was a beautiful day in Italy and I rode all afternoon around the lakes and in the arena.

"Can you ride?" I asked, trying to start the evening with a lighter vibe.

He said, "Yes, let's ride together tomorrow in the hunt."

We talked about horses, where we've ridden around the world, and the Italian breed. I asked if Saudi Arabia, Afghanistan or Pakistan has a breed. I learned there isn't one, although Afghanistan means "men on horseback."

Tonight, I decided to change strategies. Instead of focusing on shocking facts I couldn't independently verify, especially not right on the spot, I decided to attempt to persuade him to see my viewpoint as if he were a songwriter who didn't want to do a song we all wanted him to do. I had to make it *his* idea. I had to make it important to him and his family and his country to give up Osama bin Laden to the United States, even if the real devil was our own President.

I asked, "Don't you think President Kennedy would want you to arrange for Osama bin Laden to be given up to the United States in exchange for aid?"

"I spoke to [two government officials] and we can work with the next administration," he said. "But the United States cannot use a missile or a bomb and hurt civilians in Pakistan."

"What if we send a sniper?"

"They won't do that."

"Who won't do that?"

"The United States."

"Why not?" I asked. The CIA will send a sniper to kill John Lennon and Jack Kennedy but they can't figure someone out to kill Osama bin Laden?" At this point, I was thinking, 'there is *really* something wrong with this world.'

"That's within your own country's borders," Adir replied.

"But other countries use snipers so why can't we? America can do at least as much if not more than any other country, right?"

"Yes, the United States is the most powerful country in the world with the most extensive military, but they will not send a sniper to get Osama bin Laden."

"But if we drop a bomb, how do we really know he was there and he died?"

"The United States will not send a sniper," he insisted again, "it's against international laws. They've never done it before, and they won't do it now."

I still didn't buy it. "Other countries like Russia and Israel can use snipers but the most powerful country in the world is limited? That that seems a bit ridiculous, doesn't it?"

"Let me make a phone call on that," he said, noticeably frustrated. "As an American, would you want him alive or dead?"

"If I were him, I'd want to be dead. For all he has on the CIA, I'll bet they'd want him to be dead, too. I don't care as long as he's not in a position to hurt anyone anymore."

"Another problem, if he's killed, is no country will take his body," Adir said. "No one wants a shrine to a terrorist on their lawn. Not Iran, not Syria, not Saudi Arabia, or anyone else."

"Does it matter what happens to him or his body? He murdered nearly 3,000 people in New York and some of their bodies still haven't been found," I said, upset. "Cremate him and throw his ashes somewhere. I'm sorry. I don't mean to be crass, but a terrorist does not require, or in this case, deserve, a proper burial."

"You'd want an American sniper?"

"Yes, it has to be an American; otherwise people won't believe he's really dead. He's become some kind of horrible terrorist celebrity figure in the United States. Americans want him and they want him right now. If Bush doesn't get him, our next President will have to bring him to justice."

"I don't think they can do it," Adir insisted. "The United States doesn't send snipers for people like bin Laden and a missile or a bomb will kill innocent civilians in Pakistan."

"Americans are innocent civilians too and we wouldn't want other innocent people just like us to be killed or injured. The United States will send a sniper if it's the only option."

"It's against international laws," he said.

"They'll have to change them. There's the old adage that rules are made to be broken. In the court of American public opinion, no one would be upset to see this guy captured or killed."

"We'd need help with the Taliban, to stabilize the region," he said. "We need help from American troops and aid. We need schools to educate children so they don't grow up and join the Taliban in Afghanistan. The Taliban preys on uneducated kids who are vulnerable, don't have a direction and don't know where to turn. They take them in and give them a direction and they tell them that Americans wake up hating them every single day."

"First of all, that's plainly untrue," I said. "American's don't wake up hating anyone every day."

"That's what the Taliban says. It may not be true but it's what they tell those kids."

"I'm sure you'll get the help you need in aid from the United States and a herd of 12 purple stuffed elephants from Hallmark to boot if you want them. Americans want bin Laden. We want him yesterday. What I'm sure our next President won't do is give you one dollar in aid if you're not willing to figure out a way to turn Osama bin Laden over to the United States. To be honest, he's your leverage right now. I know you don't want to work with the Bush administration, and you're going to wait for an Obama Administration or Clinton Administration next but you'd better figure out a way to lock this guy up so you don't lose him because he's your ticket to get help from the United States."

"I think your next President will be Barack Obama. Hillary Clinton is running for next time. She'll be the President in eight years, after Obama."

"What if it's Hillary Clinton this time? Will you still work with her because she's a woman and I know women are treated differently in your part of the world?"

"We'll work with the Clintons. She's not just any woman and he was a better President than Bush."

I had to smile. "That's not saying much. President Clinton was the best President we've had since I've been alive."

"For Americans, that is true," he said and paused before continuing. "The Clintons have a foundation some people think is corrupt because people say a King or a Prince of a country can pay millions to the foundation and get a meeting, but I know someone who met with Hillary Clinton and they didn't get any of their agenda met with open arms."

"You mean she's not a pushover? That's good news," I smiled. "If you donate millions, I'll bet you can meet with the head of any non-profit you want. My Dad ran non-profits. I don't think there's an exception on that. Donate millions and you can meet the whole board if you want to. Doesn't the Clinton Foundation do a lot of good?"

"Yes, they do."

Changing the subject back to where we were, "So you'd be fine working with a woman to finish this deal. For sure?"

"Yes. We are coming along with rights for women. We're not as bad as Iran. You know, they banned rock music."

"Tell him (the President of Iran) that's sacrilegious in every religion!"

Adir laughed, "when you meet him, don't tell him you worked with rock bands."

"You talk. I won't tell him anything at all," I smiled.

The next morning, we met down at the barn area to participate in a drag hunt (a hunt with horses and hounds but without a fox). It was a beautiful day after so much rain that week and someone left puppies at the barn. In the lot of the playful and adorable little ones, was a very special retriever mix we were playing with as we talked further, and we decided to name him "Tala," not original at all as that apparently means "gold" in Persian. I still wonder if Adir kept him.

The Do Not Fly List

After a rainy week of riding and talks, I finally left Italy for Ireland. Ireland turned out to be another great adventure and I loved it. I've never had so much fun. The Italians and the Irish are the best in the entire world.

Unfortunately, on my last day hunting with the Galway Blazers, I came off on the very last wall and fractured my pelvis. The doctors in Ireland are so warm and kind. I was permitted to fly home but my non-stop flight was cancelled and they had to put me on a different airline with a stopover in O'Hare (nightmare in the winter). The flight landed in Chicago and there was so much snow, the connecting flight to Los Angeles was delayed until the next day. Thankfully, there was a nurse flying on the same flight. She came to the hotel and was a huge help.

The next morning, I arrived at O'Hare early because they 'lost' my luggage the night before and said it would be delivered to the hotel but it never was. Now they confirmed it was totally gone and they told me I could not fly home even though I was in a wheel chair and could barely move. The reason? Because I had been placed on the TSA 'no-fly' list by the FBI! At first, I thought they must be kidding. I was in no condition to hurt anyone and I've never owned a weapon in my life. Then I realized this was all about Italy. All about talking with Adir.

After that, I discovered the CIA monitored my e-mail for at least a couple of years when one of the forwarded e-mails bounced back (our government is bad with e-mail). No surprise, they eventually got bored and stopped reading.

Flying also became more difficult, though not impossible. I was once taken off a plane, along with a little old grandma from the Midwest and a 3-year-old child, due to the No-Fly List. Ridiculous? Thankfully, once the Obama administration took office, I didn't have any more problems.

A coincidence?

The Senate-approved $50 Million Dollar Reward

James Comey knew Osama bin Laden was living at the compound in Abbottabad by the time I spoke to Adir in 2006. But apparently, the U.S. Senate did not know or at least they knew they needed help getting access to him. In July 2007, the Senate doubled the award for Osama bin Laden's capture to $50 million.

News18.com: US Senate Doubles Bounty on Laden's Head to $50 million: http://www.news18.com/news/india/us-senate-doubles-bounty-on-ladens-head-to-50-million-269044.html [SEP]

The award reportedly has never been paid – and it should be. This should inspire other citizens to jump in where needed if they find themselves in the right or wrong place at the right or wrong time.

Since I negotiated the access for the United States to go in with a sniper team to capture or kill bin Laden, you could say that I am entitled to the reward. If I did receive the reward, I'd make sure that ¾ of the reward went to others, including a $25 million fund for 9/11 survivors, including first responders still in need, and an additional $12.5 million for nonprofit causes.

Every one of us has a vision and innate talents, but what matters most about each of our lives is what we create and leave behind for future generations. There is a world of difference I can make with that kind of money.

In Conclusion

Most people know that the United States didn't just barge into Pakistan and Afghanistan with a sniper team on May 2, 2011. Anyone with common sense would at least have an inkling that it was negotiated, carefully planned and masterfully executed on all sides. Once again, I am grateful to Hillary Clinton and President Barack Obama for keeping me a secret for this long and for allowing me to come forward in my own time.

I don't know why I persisted in debating Adir in Italy. But when I left, I felt like I won, at least for the moment. If nothing else, I won the point to keep Osama bin Laden locked up in that compound so they wouldn't lose him until the next administration could do a better job negotiating this than I did as a citizen.

On May 2, 2011, I was surprised and shocked as everyone else in America that

President Obama and Hillary Clinton got him exactly as planned and they were able to change (or maybe bend – do they do that in politics or only the music business?) the laws to capture or kill Osama bin Laden in Pakistan with a sniper team. I was grateful in the end that not only were innocent civilians protected, but the sniper team made it out alive. They are the heroes.

As I leave you, I'm still questioning myself. In my mind, this is a story that could have been left unwritten forever, but friends I've discussed it with feel otherwise. This one's for them. I hope this little book paves the beaten path for further research by women and men who have a better grasp of history than I do and a deep reinvestigation by our government into every death mentioned on behalf of all of us who call ourselves Americans. We deserve answers and we've waited way too long.

According to the King Center website, on December 8, 1999, Dr. Martin Luther King, Jr.'s family won a unanimous verdict in about an hour from 12 jurors in a civil trial. Finally, it was proven that Dr. Martin Luther King, Jr. was assassinated as a result of a conspiracy including individuals, the mafia, and 'local, state, and federal government agencies' and not by James Earl Ray. Read more here: *[The King Center: http://www.thekingcenter.org/assassination-conspiracy-trial]*

ABC News reported that Robert F. Kennedy Jr. stated publicly that if Oswald killed his uncle, he did not do it alone. *[YouTube: Robert F. Kennedy, Jr. Does Not Agree Lee Harvey Oswald Acted Alone http://abcnews.go.com/GMA/video/robert-kennedy-jr-agree-lee-harvey-oswald-acted-18201867]*

E! Online quoted Sean Lennon emphatically stating the US government killed his father: *[E! "Sean Lennon's Conspiracy Theories:" http://www.eonline.com/news/36248/sean-lennon-s-conspiracy-theories]*

Both a PBS Documentary and a Europhysics News article suggest that evidence shows the World Trade Center towers and Building 7 were destroyed by controlled demolition (which takes time to set up). The Europhysics News article concludes: "…the evidence points overwhelmingly to the conclusion that all three buildings were destroyed by controlled demolition."

[YouTube: PBS Documentary: 9/11: Explosive Evidence: Experts Speak Out – Final Edition https://www.youtube.com/watch?v=1l-8PFk8j5I]

[Europhysics News Volume 47, number 4: Article: "15 Years Later: On the Physics of High Rise Building Collapses" https://www.europhysicsnews.org/articles/epn/pdf/2016/04/epn2016-47-4.pdf]

Americans collectively need to know more about the truths of our past to better grapple with our future, especially when we have another president who stands to profit from war.

You are welcome to believe anything you want about this little book. It's a free country with free speech. But no matter what you think, please call your representatives in Congress and ask your own questions about past events, about the present, about what's happening that works for you and doesn't. Be engaged. That's what this book is about. Americans don't ask enough questions. Start asking: What are the facts? Why this agenda? Examine everything. We're not children. We deserve better than the telephone game.

Our media in the United States has come a very, very long way since the days of President Kennedy's assassination. We were once beholden to limited news footage and a print newspaper the day after such a horrific event. We had to rely on the government to tell the story, however truthful, or not so much. Even in 1980 and 1981, when John Lennon was murdered and then President Reagan was shot, we didn't have the Internet yet, at least not at most of our disposal. We were still in the dark ages.

Moving forward to 2006, we had computers and a limited version of the Internet (limited compared to today in 2017) and we were only at the start of investigative journalists having their own websites and telling truths that mainstream television networks and even newspapers wouldn't touch. The media was still towing the government line for the most part. CBS didn't stand behind their own investigative journalist, Dan Rather, because of the Bush administration. Not only was our government going to leave us believing Osama bin Laden was in a cave in Afghanistan at the time (where he wasn't), but they were set on dictating who could talk to us about that cave!

Thankfully, it's 11 years later and there have been great strides toward reporting the truth to Americans if for no other reason than the truth gets great ratings! When Donald Trump lies and says, "I didn't say that," we all love Rachel Maddow for showing us clips of three times he *did* say exactly what he swears he never said. Americans want politicians called out on their lies.

We need our press to be free so we can be informed. When Donald Trump lied and called *The New York Times* 'fake news,' they responded with their greatest, most truthful, most engaging journalism ever and so did their colleagues at *The Washington Post, Los Angeles Times*, and other major papers.

To add to the experience, the Internet is now an incredible research tool. Information that would take years to investigate and compile in the 60s, 70s, and 80s is now hiding in plain sight on Wikipedia. And, regular citizens like you and I can read news, report news, ask questions, and even tag our favorite television host and tell him we love his purple tie and his non-profit work. Although I don't agree that Twitter is a good format for foreign policy correspondence in 140 characters (who would have thought?), I love that it is now possible to use Twitter and Facebook to communicate with politicians, some of whom actually read regular people's comments and concerns.

To Adir, I will forever be grateful for your time, for your patience, and for your willingness to listen so thoughtfully to a stranger and an ordinary American citizen. Even though I could do nothing or change anything, you made me realize that we can all do something. I learned so much, maybe too much, but I've given every word more thought, more time, and now that we have a full-fledged internet complete with encyclopedias and independent journalists' websites to read internationally for new and alternative perspectives, it's been an adventure and a journey that only started at the little table in the corner of the bar in Italy. You wanted to know "Why don't Americans ask questions? Why don't we make demands on our government? Why don't we put two and two together when the government tells us a story that is obviously untrue?" Now in 2017, as Americans, we're answering those questions and we're finally moving toward a more engaged populace because we have to. And you're right – it's about time.

Last, Friends, I leave you to ponder this short book, Always Face the Hounds. Face whatever is in front of you. When you're on a horse, you are forced to look where you're going and you're constantly responding to what is in your path. When you're not on a horse, you can look the other way and avoid, procrastinate and do something else for a while but everything you face will come back to you again if you don't face it now. History repeats itself and we all need to look back to look forward. It might be a slightly different situation and different people but we'll keep experiencing the same set of circumstances again and again until we face what's happening, and change our strategy so that the ending works for everyone.

Let's start by asking once again:

Should an American president and his family profit from sending the United States into a war?

Peace.

Meghan Hansen

Meghan is a music executive with over 20 years of experience working with well-known and developing artists. She has worked for major labels at Universal Music Group including Universal Republic Records and Geffen Records, and Sony Music Entertainment including Columbia Records. Meghan holds a Bachelor of Arts in Liberal Arts/Media Studies from The New School for Social Research in New York, NY. She currently lives in Malibu, California.

Your thoughts are appreciated! Please consider reviewing Always Face the Hounds on Amazon.com: <u>www.alwaysfacethehounds.com</u>

And feel free to visit and start or join a discussion on the Always Face the Hounds Facebook page at <u>www.facebook.com/alwaysfacethehounds</u>

To write to the author, Meghan Hansen, please e-mail <u>meghansen90265@gmail.com</u>.